PLATO'S
MENO

PLATO'S
MENO

Translated by:
BENJAMIN JOWETT

Publishers, LLC

ROCKVILLE, MARYLAND
2010

ISBN: 978-1-60450-781-2

NOTE FOR TEACHERS

Serenity Publishers can custom create classic texts for your classes

We can create new titles with special pricing and margins

Add your notes and create the book to your exact specifications

Combine different classic texts in one volume

Produce an edition with a special introduction or an afterword

Add your footnotes

Visit **www.SerenityPublishers.com** & **www.ManorStudent.com** or email **chandi@serenitypublishers.com**

Published by Serenity Publishers
An Arc Manor Company
P. O. Box 10339
Rockville, MD 20849-0339
www.SerenityPublishers.com

Printed in the United States of America/United Kingdom

INTRODUCTION

This Dialogue begins abruptly with a question of Meno, who asks, 'whether virtue can be taught.' Socrates replies that he does not as yet know what virtue is, and has never known anyone who did. 'Then he cannot have met Gorgias when he was at Athens.' Yes, Socrates had met him, but he has a bad memory, and has forgotten what Gorgias said. Will Meno tell him his own notion, which is probably not very different from that of Gorgias? 'O yes—nothing easier: there is the virtue of a man, of a woman, of an old man, and of a child; there is a virtue of every age and state of life, all of which may be easily described.'

Socrates reminds Meno that this is only an enumeration of the virtues and not a definition of the notion which is common to them all. In a second attempt Meno defines virtue to be 'the power of command.' But to this, again, exceptions are taken. For there must be a virtue of those who obey, as well as of those who command; and the power of command must be justly or not unjustly exercised. Meno is very ready to admit that justice is virtue: 'Would you say virtue or a virtue, for there are other virtues, such as courage, temperance, and the like; just as round is a figure, and black and white are colours, and yet there are other figures and other colours. Let Meno take the examples of figure and colour, and try to define them.' Meno confesses his inability, and after a process of interrogation, in which Socrates explains to him the nature of a 'simile in multis,' Socrates himself defines figure as 'the accompaniment of colour.' But some one may object that he does not know the meaning of the word 'colour;' and if he is a candid friend, and not a mere disputant, Socrates is willing to furnish him with a simpler and more philosophical definition, into which no disputed word is allowed to intrude: 'Figure is the limit of form.' Meno imperiously insists that he must still have a definition of colour. Some raillery follows; and at length Socrates is induced to reply, 'that colour is the effluence of form, sensible, and in due proportion to the sight.' This definition is exactly suited to the taste of Meno, who welcomes the familiar language of Gorgias and Empedocles. Socrates is of opinion that the more abstract or dialectical definition of figure is far better.

Now that Meno has been made to understand the nature of a general definition, he answers in the spirit of a Greek gentleman, and in the words of a poet, 'that virtue is to delight in things honourable, and to have the power of getting them.' This is a nearer approximation than he has yet made to a complete definition, and, regarded as a piece of proverbial or popular morality, is not far from the truth. But the objection is urged, 'that the honourable is the good,' and as every one equally desires the good, the point of the definition is contained in the words, 'the power of getting them.' 'And they must be got justly or with justice.' The definition will then stand thus: 'Virtue is the power of getting good with justice.' But justice is a part of virtue, and therefore virtue is the getting of good with a part of virtue. The definition repeats the word defined.

Meno complains that the conversation of Socrates has the effect of a torpedo's shock upon him. When he talks with other persons he has plenty to say about virtue; in the presence of Socrates, his thoughts desert him. Socrates replies that he is only the cause of perplexity in others, because he is himself perplexed. He proposes to continue the enquiry. But how, asks Meno, can he enquire either into what he knows or into what he does not know? This is a sophistical puzzle, which, as Socrates remarks, saves a great deal of trouble to him who accepts it. But the puzzle has a real difficulty latent under it, to which Socrates will endeavour to find a reply. The difficulty is the origin of knowledge:—

He has heard from priests and priestesses, and from the poet Pindar, of an immortal soul which is born again and again in successive periods of existence, returning into this world when she has paid the penalty of ancient crime, and, having wandered over all places of the upper and under world, and seen and known all things at one time or other, is by association out of one thing capable of recovering all. For nature is of one kindred; and every soul has a seed or germ which may be developed into all knowledge. The existence of this latent knowledge is further proved by the interrogation of one of Meno's slaves, who, in the skilful hands of Socrates, is made to acknowledge some elementary relations of geometrical figures. The theorem that the square of the diagonal is double the square of the side— that famous discovery of primitive mathematics, in honour of which the legendary Pythagoras is said to have sacrificed a hecatomb—is elicited from him. The first step in the process of teaching has made him conscious of his own ignorance. He has had the 'torpedo's shock' given him, and is the better for the operation. But whence had the uneducated man this knowledge? He had never learnt geometry in this world; nor was it born with him; he must therefore have had it when he was not a man. And as he always either was or was not a man, he must have always had it. (Compare Phaedo.)

After Socrates has given this specimen of the true nature of teaching, the original question of the teachableness of virtue is renewed. Again he professes a desire to know 'what virtue is' first. But he is willing to argue the question, as mathematicians say, under an hypothesis. He will assume that if virtue is knowledge, then virtue can be taught. (This was the stage of the argument at which the Protagoras concluded.)

Socrates has no difficulty in showing that virtue is a good, and that goods, whether of body or mind, must be under the direction of knowledge. Upon the assumption just made, then, virtue is teachable. But where are the teachers? There are none to be found. This is extremely discouraging. Virtue is no sooner discovered to be teachable, than the discovery follows that it is not taught. Virtue, therefore, is and is not teachable.

In this dilemma an appeal is made to Anytus, a respectable and well-to-do citizen of the old school, and a family friend of Meno, who happens to be present. He is asked 'whether Meno shall go to the Sophists and be taught.' The suggestion throws him into a rage. 'To whom, then, shall Meno go?' asks Socrates. To any Athenian gentleman—to the great Athenian statesmen of past times. Socrates replies here, as elsewhere (Laches, Prot.), that Themistocles, Pericles, and other great men, had sons to whom they would surely, if they could have done so, have imparted their own political wisdom; but no one ever heard that these sons of theirs were remarkable for anything except riding and wrestling and similar accomplishments. Anytus is angry at the imputation which is cast on his favourite statesmen, and on a class to which he supposes himself to belong; he breaks off with a significant hint. The mention of another opportunity of talking with him, and the suggestion that Meno may do the Athenian people a service by pacifying him, are evident allusions to the trial of Socrates.

Socrates returns to the consideration of the question 'whether virtue is teachable,' which was denied on the ground that there are no teachers of it: (for the Sophists are bad teachers, and the rest of the world do not profess to teach). But there is another point which we failed to observe, and in which Gorgias has never instructed Meno, nor Prodicus Socrates. This is the nature of right opinion. For virtue may be under the guidance of right opinion as well as of knowledge; and right opinion is for practical purposes as good as knowledge, but is incapable of being taught, and is also liable, like the images of Daedalus, to 'walk off,' because not bound by the tie of the cause. This is the sort of instinct which is possessed by statesmen, who are not wise or knowing persons, but only inspired or divine. The higher virtue, which is identical with knowledge, is an ideal only. If the statesman had this knowledge, and could teach what he knew, he would be like Tiresias in the world below,—'he alone has wisdom, but the rest flit like shadows.'

This Dialogue is an attempt to answer the question, Can virtue be taught? No one would either ask or answer such a question in modern times. But in the age of Socrates it was only by an effort that the mind could rise to a general notion of virtue as distinct from the particular virtues of courage, liberality, and the like. And when a hazy conception of this ideal was attained, it was only by a further effort that the question of the teachableness of virtue could be resolved.

The answer which is given by Plato is paradoxical enough, and seems rather intended to stimulate than to satisfy enquiry. Virtue is knowledge, and therefore virtue can be taught. But virtue is not taught, and therefore in this higher and ideal sense there is no virtue and no knowledge. The teaching of the Sophists is confessedly inadequate, and Meno, who is their pupil, is ignorant of the very nature of general terms. He can only produce out of their armoury the sophism, 'that you can neither enquire into what you know nor into what you do not know;' to which Socrates replies by his theory of reminiscence.

To the doctrine that virtue is knowledge, Plato has been constantly tending in the previous Dialogues. But the new truth is no sooner found than it vanishes away. 'If there is knowledge, there must be teachers; and where are the teachers?' There is no knowledge in the higher sense of systematic, connected, reasoned knowledge, such as may one day be attained, and such as Plato himself seems to see in some far off vision of a single science. And there are no teachers in the higher sense of the word; that is to say, no real teachers who will arouse the spirit of enquiry in their pupils, and not merely instruct them in rhetoric or impart to them ready-made information for a fee of 'one' or of 'fifty drachms.' Plato is desirous of deepening the notion of education, and therefore he asserts the paradox that there are no educators. This paradox, though different in form, is not really different from the remark which is often made in modern times by those who would depreciate either the methods of education commonly employed, or the standard attained—that 'there is no true education among us.'

There remains still a possibility which must not be overlooked. Even if there be no true knowledge, as is proved by 'the wretched state of education,' there may be right opinion, which is a sort of guessing or divination resting on no knowledge of causes, and incommunicable to others. This is the gift which our statesmen have, as is proved by the circumstance that they are unable to impart their knowledge to their sons. Those who are possessed of it cannot be said to be men of science or philosophers, but they are inspired and divine.

There may be some trace of irony in this curious passage, which forms the concluding portion of the Dialogue. But Plato certainly does not mean to intimate that the supernatural or divine is the true basis of human life. To him knowledge, if only attainable in this world, is of all things the most divine. Yet, like other philosophers, he is willing to admit that 'probability is the guide of life (Butler's Analogy.);' and he is at the same time desirous of contrasting the wisdom which governs the world with a higher wisdom. There are many instincts, judgments, and anticipations of the human mind which cannot be reduced to rule, and of which the grounds cannot always be given in words. A person may have some skill or latent experience which he is able to use himself and is yet unable to teach others, because he has no principles, and is incapable of collecting or arranging his ideas. He has practice, but not theory; art, but not science. This is a true fact of psychology, which is recognized by Plato in this passage. But he is far from saying, as some have imagined, that inspiration or divine grace is to be regarded as higher than knowledge. He would not have preferred the poet or man of action to the philosopher, or the virtue of custom to the virtue based upon ideas.

Also here, as in the Ion and Phaedrus, Plato appears to acknowledge an unreasoning element in the higher nature of man. The philosopher only has knowledge, and yet the statesman and the poet are inspired. There may be a sort of irony in regarding in this way the gifts of genius. But there is no reason to suppose that he is deriding them, any more than he is deriding the phenomena of love or of enthusiasm in the Symposium, or of oracles in the Apology, or of divine intimations when he is speaking of the daemonium of Socrates. He recognizes the lower form of right opinion, as well as the higher one of science, in the spirit of one who desires to include in his philosophy every aspect of human life; just as he recognizes the existence of popular opinion as a fact, and the Sophists as the expression of it.

This Dialogue contains the first intimation of the doctrine of reminiscence and of the immortality of the soul. The proof is very slight, even slighter than in the Phaedo and Republic. Because men had abstract ideas in a previous state, they must have always had them, and their souls therefore must have always existed. For they must always have been either men or not men. The fallacy of the latter words is transparent. And Socrates himself appears to be conscious of their weakness; for he adds immediately afterwards, 'I have said some things of which I am not altogether confident.' (Compare Phaedo.) It may be observed, however, that the fanciful notion of pre-existence is combined with a true but partial view of the origin and unity of knowledge, and of the association of ideas. Knowledge is prior to any particular knowledge, and exists not in the previous state of the individual, but of the race. It is potential, not actual, and can only be appropriated by strenuous exertion.

The idealism of Plato is here presented in a less developed form than in the Phaedo and Phaedrus. Nothing is said of the pre-existence of ideas of justice, temperance, and the like. Nor is Socrates positive of anything but the duty of enquiry. The doctrine of reminiscence too is explained more in accordance with fact and experience as arising out of the affinities of nature (ate tes thuseos oles suggenous ouses). Modern philosophy says that all things in nature are dependent on one another; the ancient philosopher had the same truth latent in his mind when he affirmed that out of one thing all the rest may be recovered. The subjective was converted by him into an objective; the mental phenomenon of the association of ideas (compare Phaedo) became a real chain of existences. The germs of two valuable principles of education may also be gathered from the 'words of priests and priestesses:' (1) that true knowledge is a knowledge of causes (compare Aristotle's theory of episteme); and (2) that the process of learning consists not in what is brought to the learner, but in what is drawn out of him.

Some lesser points of the dialogue may be noted, such as (1) the acute observation that Meno prefers the familiar definition, which is embellished with poetical language, to the better and truer one; or (2) the shrewd reflection, which may admit of an application to modern as well as to ancient teachers, that the Sophists having made large fortunes; this must surely be a criterion of their powers of teaching, for that no man could get a living by shoemaking who was not a good shoemaker; or (3) the remark conveyed, almost in a word, that the verbal sceptic is saved the labour of thought and enquiry (ouden dei to toiouto zeteseos). Characteristic also of the temper of the Socratic enquiry is, (4) the proposal to discuss the teachableness of virtue under an hypothesis, after the manner of the mathematicians; and (5) the repetition of the favourite doctrine which occurs so frequently in the earlier and more Socratic Dialogues, and gives a colour to all of them—that mankind only desire evil through ignorance; (6) the experiment of eliciting from the slave-boy the mathematical truth which is latent in him, and (7) the remark that he is all the better for knowing his ignorance.

The character of Meno, like that of Critias, has no relation to the actual circumstances of his life. Plato is silent about his treachery to the ten thousand Greeks, which Xenophon has recorded, as he is also silent about the crimes of Critias. He is a Thessalian Alcibiades, rich and luxurious—a spoilt child of fortune, and is described as the hereditary friend of the great king. Like Alcibiades he is inspired with an ardent desire of knowledge, and is equally willing to learn of Socrates and of the Sophists. He may be regarded as standing in the same relation to Gorgias as Hippocrates in the Protagoras to the other great Sophist. He is the sophisticated youth on whom Socrates tries his cross-examining powers, just as in the Charmides, the Lysis, and the Euthydemus, ingenuous boyhood is made the subject of a similar experiment. He is treated by Socrates in a half-playful manner suited to his character; at the same time he appears not quite to understand the process to which he is being subjected. For he is exhibited as ignorant of the very elements of dialectics, in which the Sophists have failed to instruct their disciple. His definition of virtue as 'the power and desire of attaining things honourable,' like the first definition of justice in the Republic, is taken from a poet. His answers have a sophistical ring, and at the same time show the sophistical incapacity to grasp a general notion.

Anytus is the type of the narrow-minded man of the
world, who is indignant at innovation, and equally
detests the popular teacher and the true philosopher. He seems, like Aristophanes, to regard the
new opinions, whether of Socrates or the Sophists,
as fatal to Athenian greatness. He is of the same
class as Callicles in the Gorgias, but of a different
variety; the immoral and sophistical doctrines of
Callicles are not attributed to him. The moderation
with which he is described is remarkable, if he be
the accuser of Socrates, as is apparently indicated
by his parting words. Perhaps Plato may have been
desirous of showing that the accusation of Socrates
was not to be attributed to badness or malevolence,
but rather to a tendency in men's minds. Or he may
have been regardless of the historical truth of the
characters of his dialogue, as in the case of Meno
and Critias. Like Chaerephon (Apol.) the real Anytus was a democrat, and had joined Thrasybulus in
the conflict with the thirty.

The Protagoras arrived at a sort of hypothetical
conclusion, that if 'virtue is knowledge, it can be
taught.' In the Euthydemus, Socrates himself of-
fered an example of the manner in which the true
teacher may draw out the mind of youth; this was
in contrast to the quibbling follies of the Sophists. In the Meno the subject is more developed;
the foundations of the enquiry are laid deeper,
and the nature of knowledge is more distinctly
explained. There is a progression by antagonism
of two opposite aspects of philosophy. But at the
moment when we approach nearest, the truth
doubles upon us and passes out of our reach. We
seem to find that the ideal of knowledge is irrec-
oncilable with experience. In human life there
is indeed the profession of knowledge, but right
opinion is our actual guide. There is another sort
of progress from the general notions of Socrates,

who asked simply, 'what is friendship?' 'what is temperance?' 'what is courage?' as in the Lysis, Charmides, Laches, to the transcendentalism of Plato, who, in the second stage of his philosophy, sought to find the nature of knowledge in a prior and future state of existence.

The difficulty in framing general notions which has appeared in this and in all the previous Dialogues recurs in the Gorgias and Theaetetus as well as in the Republic. In the Gorgias too the statesmen reappear, but in stronger opposition to the philosopher. They are no longer allowed to have a divine insight, but, though acknowledged to have been clever men and good speakers, are denounced as 'blind leaders of the blind.' The doctrine of the immortality of the soul is also carried further, being made the foundation not only of a theory of knowledge, but of a doctrine of rewards and punishments. In the Republic the relation of knowledge to virtue is described in a manner more consistent with modern distinctions. The existence of the virtues without the possession of knowledge in the higher or philosophical sense is admitted to be possible. Right opinion is again introduced in the Theaetetus as an account of knowledge, but is rejected on the ground that it is irrational (as here, because it is not bound by the tie of the cause), and also because the conception of false opinion is given up as hopeless. The doctrines of Plato are necessarily different at different times of his life, as new distinctions are realized, or new stages of thought attained by him. We are not therefore justified, in order to take away the appearance of inconsistency, in attributing to him hidden meanings or remote allusions.

There are no external criteria by which we can determine the date of the Meno. There is no reason to suppose that any of the Dialogues of Plato were written before the death of Socrates; the Meno, which appears to be one of the earliest of them, is proved to have been of a later date by the allusion of Anytus.

We cannot argue that Plato was more likely to have written, as he has done, of Meno before than after his miserable death; for we have already seen, in the examples of Charmides and Critias, that the characters in Plato are very far from resembling the same characters in history. The repulsive picture which is given of him in the Anabasis of Xenophon, where he also appears as the friend of Aristippus 'and a fair youth having lovers,' has no other trait of likeness to the Meno of Plato.

The place of the Meno in the series is doubtfully indicated by internal evidence. The main character of the Dialogue is Socrates; but to the 'general definitions' of Socrates is added the Platonic doctrine of reminiscence. The problems of virtue and knowledge have been discussed in the Lysis, Laches, Charmides, and Protagoras; the puzzle about knowing and learning has already appeared in the Euthydemus. The doctrines of immortality and pre-existence are carried further in the Phaedrus and Phaedo; the distinction between opinion and knowledge is more fully developed in the Theaetetus. The lessons of Prodicus, whom he facetiously calls his master, are still running in the mind of Socrates. Unlike the later Platonic Dialogues, the Meno arrives at no conclusion. Hence we are led to place the Dialogue at some point of time later than the Protagoras, and earlier than the Phaedrus and Gorgias. The place which is assigned to it in this work is due mainly to the desire to bring together in a single volume all the Dialogues which contain allusions to the trial and death of Socrates.

ooooo

ON THE IDEAS OF PLATO

Plato's doctrine of ideas has attained an imaginary clearness and definiteness which is not to be found in his own writings. The popular account of them is partly derived from one or two passages in his Dialogues interpreted without regard to their poetical environment. It is due also to the misunderstanding of him by the Aristotelian school; and the erroneous notion has been further narrowed and has become fixed by the realism of the schoolmen. This popular view of the Platonic ideas may be summed up in some such formula as the following: 'Truth consists not in particulars, but in universals, which have a place in the mind of God, or in some far-off heaven. These were revealed to men in a former state of existence, and are recovered by reminiscence (anamnesis) or association from sensible things. The sensible things are not realities, but shadows only, in relation to the truth.' These unmeaning propositions are hardly suspected to be a caricature of a great theory of knowledge, which Plato in various ways and under many figures of speech is seeking to unfold. Poetry has been converted into dogma; and it is not remarked that the Platonic ideas are to be found only in about a third of Plato's writings and are not confined to him. The forms which they assume are numerous, and if taken literally, inconsistent with one another. At one time we are in the clouds of mythology, at another among the abstractions of mathematics or metaphysics; we pass imperceptibly from one to the other. Reason and fancy are mingled in the same passage. The ideas are sometimes described as many, coextensive with the universals of sense and also with the first principles of ethics; or again they are absorbed into the single idea of good, and subordinated to it. They are not more certain than facts, but they are equally certain (Phaedo). They are both personal and impersonal. They are abstract terms: they are also the causes of things; and they are even transformed into the demons or spirits by whose help God made the world. And the idea of good (Republic) may without violence be converted into the Supreme Being, who 'because He was good' created all things (Tim.).

It would be a mistake to try and reconcile these differing modes of thought. They are not to be regarded seriously as having a distinct meaning. They are parables, prophecies, myths, symbols, revelations, aspirations after an unknown world. They derive their origin from a deep religious and contemplative feeling, and also from an observation of curious mental phenomena. They gather up the elements of the previous philosophies, which they put together in a new form. Their great diversity shows the tentative character of early endeavours to think. They have not yet settled down into a single system. Plato uses them, though he also criticises them; he acknowledges that both he and others are always talking about them, especially about the Idea of Good; and that they are not peculiar to himself (Phaedo; Republic; Soph.). But in his later writings he seems to have laid aside the old forms of them. As he proceeds he makes for himself new modes of expression more akin to the Aristotelian logic.

Yet amid all these varieties and incongruities, there is a common meaning or spirit which pervades his writings, both those in which he treats of the ideas and those in which he is silent about them. This is the spirit of idealism, which in the history of philosophy has had many names and taken many forms, and has in a measure influenced those who seemed to be most averse to it. It has often been charged with inconsistency and fancifulness, and yet has had an elevating effect on human nature, and has exercised a wonderful charm and interest over a few spirits who have been lost in the thought of it. It has been banished again and again, but has always returned. It has attempted to leave the earth and soar heavenwards, but soon has found that only in experience could any solid foundation of knowledge be laid. It has degenerated into pantheism, but has again emerged. No other knowledge has given an equal stimulus to the mind. It is the science of sciences, which are also ideas, and under either aspect require to be defined. They can only be thought of in due proportion when conceived in relation to one another. They are the glasses through which the kingdoms of science are seen, but at a distance. All the greatest minds, except when living in an age of reaction against them, have unconsciously fallen under their power.

The account of the Platonic ideas in the Meno is the simplest and clearest, and we shall best illustrate their nature by giving this first and then comparing the manner in which they are described elsewhere, e.g. in the Phaedrus, Phaedo, Republic; to which may be added the criticism of them in the Parmenides, the personal form which is attributed to them in the Timaeus, the logical character which they assume in the Sophist and Philebus, and the allusion to them in the Laws. In the Cratylus they dawn upon him with the freshness of a newly-discovered thought.

The Meno goes back to a former state of existence, in which men did and suffered good and evil, and received the reward or punishment of them until their sin was purged away and they were allowed to return to earth. This is a tradition of the olden time, to which priests and poets bear witness. The souls of men returning to earth bring back a latent memory of ideas, which were known to them in a former state. The recollection is awakened into life and consciousness by the sight of the things which resemble them on earth. The soul evidently possesses such innate ideas before she has had time to acquire them. This is proved by an experiment tried on one of Meno's slaves, from whom Socrates elicits truths of arithmetic and geometry, which he had never learned in this world. He must therefore have brought them with him from another.

The notion of a previous state of existence is found in the verses of Empedocles and in the fragments of Heracleitus. It was the natural answer to two questions, 'Whence came the soul? What is the origin of evil?' and prevailed far and wide in the east. It found its way into Hellas probably through the medium of Orphic and Pythagorean rites and mysteries. It was easier to think of a former than of a future life, because such a life has really existed for the race though not for the individual, and all men come into the world, if not 'trailing clouds of glory,' at any rate able to enter into the inheritance of the past. In the Phaedrus, as well as in the Meno, it is this former rather than a future life on which Plato is disposed to dwell. There the Gods, and men following in their train, go forth to contemplate the heavens, and are borne round in the revolutions of them. There they see the divine forms of justice, temperance, and the like, in their unchangeable beauty, but not without an effort more than human. The soul of man is likened to a charioteer and two steeds, one mortal, the other immortal. The charioteer and the mortal steed are in fierce conflict; at length the animal principle is finally overpowered, though not extinguished, by the combined energies of the passionate and rational elements. This is one of those passages in Plato which, partaking both of a philosophical and poetical character, is necessarily indistinct and inconsistent. The magnificent figure under which the nature of the soul is described has not much to do with the popular doctrine of the ideas. Yet there is one little trait in the description which shows that they are present to Plato's mind, namely, the remark that the soul, which had seen truths in the form of the universal, cannot again return to the nature of an animal.

In the Phaedo, as in the Meno, the origin of ideas is sought for in a previous state of existence. There was no time when they could have been acquired in this life, and therefore they must have been recovered from another. The process of recovery is no other than the ordinary law of association, by which in daily life the sight of one thing or person recalls another to our minds, and by which in scientific enquiry from any part of knowledge we may be led on to infer the whole. It is also argued that ideas, or rather ideals, must be derived from a previous state of existence because they are more perfect than the sensible forms of them which are given by experience. But in the Phaedo the doctrine of ideas is subordinate to the proof of the immortality of the soul. 'If the soul existed in a previous state, then it will exist in a future state, for a law of alternation pervades all things.' And, 'If the ideas exist, then the soul exists; if not, not.' It is to be observed, both in the Meno and the Phaedo, that Socrates expresses himself with diffidence. He speaks in the Phaedo of the words with which he has comforted himself and his friends, and will not be too confident that the description which he has given of the soul and her mansions is exactly true, but he 'ventures to think that something of the kind is true.' And in the Meno, after dwelling upon the immortality of the soul, he adds, 'Of some things which I have said I am not altogether confident' (compare Apology; Gorgias). From this class of uncertainties he exempts the difference between truth and appearance, of which he is absolutely convinced.

In the Republic the ideas are spoken of in two ways, which though not contradictory are different. In the tenth book they are represented as the genera or general ideas under which individuals having a common name are contained. For example, there is the bed which the carpenter makes, the picture of the bed which is drawn by the painter, the bed existing in nature of which God is the author. Of the latter all visible beds are only the shadows or reflections. This and similar illustrations or explanations are put forth, not for their own sake, or as an exposition of Plato's theory of ideas, but with a view of showing that poetry and the mimetic arts are concerned with an inferior part of the soul and a lower kind of knowledge. On the other hand, in the 6th and 7th books of the Republic we reach the highest and most perfect conception, which Plato is able to attain, of the nature of knowledge. The ideas are now finally seen to be one as well as many, causes as well as ideas, and to have a unity which is the idea of good and the cause of all the rest. They seem, however, to have lost their first aspect of universals under which individuals are contained, and to have been converted into forms of another kind, which are inconsistently regarded from the one side as images or ideals of justice, temperance, holiness and the like; from the other as hypotheses, or mathematical truths or principles.

In the Timaeus, which in the series of Plato's works immediately follows the Republic, though probably written some time afterwards, no mention occurs of the doctrine of ideas. Geometrical forms and arithmetical ratios furnish the laws according to which the world is created. But though the conception of the ideas as genera or species is forgotten or laid aside, the distinction of the visible and intellectual is as firmly maintained as ever. The *idea* of good likewise disappears and is superseded by the conception of a personal God, who works according to a final cause or principle of goodness which he himself is. No doubt is expressed by Plato, either in the Timaeus or in any other dialogue, of the truths which he conceives to be the first and highest. It is not the existence of God or the idea of good which he approaches in a tentative or hesitating manner, but the investigations of physiology. These he regards, not seriously, as a part of philosophy, but as an innocent recreation (Tim.).

Passing on to the Parmenides, we find in that dialogue not an exposition or defence of the doctrine of ideas, but an assault upon them, which is put into the mouth of the veteran Parmenides, and might be ascribed to Aristotle himself, or to one of his disciples. The doctrine which is assailed takes two or three forms, but fails in any of them to escape the dialectical difficulties which are urged against it. It is admitted that there are ideas of all things, but the manner in which individuals partake of them, whether of the whole or of the part, and in which they become like them, or how ideas can be either within or without the sphere of human knowledge, or how the human and divine can have any relation to each other, is held to be incapable of explanation. And yet, if there are no universal ideas, what becomes of philosophy? (Parmenides.) In the Sophist the theory of ideas is spoken of as a doctrine held not by Plato, but by another sect of philosophers, called 'the Friends of Ideas,' probably the Megarians, who were very distinct from him, if not opposed to him (Sophist). Nor in what may be termed Plato's abridgement of the history of philosophy (Soph.), is any mention made such as we find in the first book of Aristotle's Metaphysics, of the derivation of such a theory or of any part of it from the Pythagoreans, the Eleatics, the Heracleiteans, or even from Socrates. In the Philebus, probably one of the latest of the Platonic Dialogues, the conception of a personal or semi-personal deity expressed under the figure of mind, the king of all, who is also the cause, is retained. The one and many of the Phaedrus and Theaetetus is still working in the mind of Plato, and the correlation of ideas, not of 'all with all,' but of 'some with some,' is asserted and explained. But they are spoken of in a different manner, and are not supposed to be recovered from a former state of existence. The metaphysical conception of truth passes into a psychological one, which is continued in the Laws, and is the final form of the Platonic philosophy, so far as can be gathered from his own writings (see especially Laws). In the Laws he harps once more on the old string, and returns to general notions:—these he acknowledges to be many, and yet he insists that they are also one. The guardian must be made to recognize the truth, for which he has contended long ago in the Protagoras, that the virtues are four, but they are also in some sense one (Laws; compare Protagoras).

So various, and if regarded on the surface only, inconsistent, are the statements of Plato respecting the doctrine of ideas. If we attempted to harmonize or to combine them, we should make out of them, not a system, but the caricature of a system. They are the ever-varying expression of Plato's Idealism. The terms used in them are in their substance and general meaning the same, although they seem to be different. They pass from the subject to the object, from earth (diesseits) to heaven (jenseits) without regard to the gulf which later theology and philosophy have made between them. They are also intended to supplement or explain each other. They relate to a subject of which Plato himself would have said that 'he was not confident of the precise form of his own statements, but was strong in the belief that something of the kind was true.' It is the spirit, not the letter, in which they agree—the spirit which places the divine above the human, the spiritual above the material, the one above the many, the mind before the body.

The stream of ancient philosophy in the Alexandrian and Roman times widens into a lake or sea, and then disappears underground to reappear after many ages in a distant land. It begins to flow again under new conditions, at first confined between high and narrow banks, but finally spreading over the continent of Europe. It is and is not the same with ancient philosophy. There is a great deal in modern philosophy which is inspired by ancient. There is much in ancient philosophy which was 'born out of due time; and before men were capable of understanding it. To the fathers of modern philosophy, their own thoughts appeared to be new and original, but they carried with them an echo or shadow of the past, coming back by recollection from an elder world. Of this the enquirers of the seventeenth century, who to themselves appeared to be working out independently the enquiry into all truth, were unconscious. They stood in a new relation to theology and natural philosophy, and for a time maintained towards both an attitude of reserve and separation. Yet the similarities between modern and ancient thought are greater far than the differences. All philosophy, even that part of it which is said to be based upon experience, is really ideal; and ideas are not only derived from facts, but they are also prior to them and extend far beyond them, just as the mind is prior to the senses.

Early Greek speculation culminates in the ideas of Plato, or rather in the single idea of good. His followers, and perhaps he himself, having arrived at this elevation, instead of going forwards went backwards from philosophy to psychology, from ideas to numbers. But what we perceive to be the real meaning of them, an explanation of the nature and origin of knowledge, will always continue to be one of the first problems of philosophy.

Plato also left behind him a most potent instrument, the forms of logic—arms ready for use, but not yet taken out of their armoury. They were the late birth of the early Greek philosophy, and were the only part of it which has had an uninterrupted hold on the mind of Europe. Philosophies come and go; but the detection of fallacies, the framing of definitions, the invention of methods still continue to be the main elements of the reasoning process.

Modern philosophy, like ancient, begins with very simple conceptions. It is almost wholly a reflection on self. It might be described as a quickening into life of old words and notions latent in the semi-barbarous Latin, and putting a new meaning into them. Unlike ancient philosophy, it has been unaffected by impressions derived from outward nature: it arose within the limits of the mind itself. From the time of Descartes to Hume and Kant it has had little or nothing to do with facts of science. On the other hand, the ancient and mediaeval logic retained a continuous influence over it, and a form like that of mathematics was easily impressed upon it; the principle of ancient philosophy which is most apparent in it is scepticism;

we must doubt nearly every traditional or received notion, that we may hold fast one or two. The being of God in a personal or impersonal form was a mental necessity to the first thinkers of modern times: from this alone all other ideas could be deduced. There had been an obscure presentiment of 'cognito, ergo sum' more than 2000 years previously. The Eleatic notion that being and thought were the same was revived in a new form by Descartes. But now it gave birth to consciousness and self-reflection: it awakened the 'ego' in human nature. The mind naked and abstract has no other certainty but the conviction of its own existence. 'I think, therefore I am;' and this thought is God thinking in me, who has also communicated to the reason of man his own attributes of thought and extension—these are truly imparted to him because God is true (compare Republic). It has been often remarked that Descartes, having begun by dismissing all presuppositions, introduces several: he passes almost at once from scepticism to dogmatism. It is more important for the illustration of Plato to observe that he, like Plato, insists that God is true and incapable of deception (Republic)—that he proceeds from general ideas, that many elements of mathematics may be found in him. A certain influence of mathematics both on the form and substance of their philosophy is discernible in both of them. After making the greatest opposition between thought and extension, Descartes, like Plato, supposes them to be reunited for a time, not in their own nature but by a special divine act (compare Phaedrus), and he also supposes all the parts of the human body to meet in the pineal gland, that alone affording a principle of unity in the material frame of man. It is characteristic of the first period of modern philosophy, that having begun (like the Presocratics) with a few general notions, Descartes first falls absolutely under their influence, and then quickly discards them. At the same time he is less able to observe facts, because they are too much magnified by the glasses through which they are seen. The common logic says 'the greater the extension, the less the comprehension,' and we may put the same thought in another way and say of abstract or general ideas, that the greater the abstraction of them, the less are they capable of being applied to particular and concrete natures.

Not very different from Descartes in his relation to ancient philosophy is his successor Spinoza, who lived in the following generation. The system of Spinoza is less personal and also less dualistic than that of Descartes. In this respect the difference between them is like that between Xenophanes and Parmenides. The teaching of Spinoza might be described generally as the Jewish religion reduced to an abstraction and taking the form of the Eleatic philosophy. Like Parmenides, he is overpowered and intoxicated with the idea of Being or God. The greatness of both philosophies consists in the immensity of a thought which excludes all other thoughts; their weakness is the necessary separation of this thought from actual existence and from practical life. In neither of them is there any clear opposition between the inward and outward world. The substance of Spinoza has two attributes, which alone are cognizable by man, thought and extension; these are in extreme opposition to one another, and also in inseparable identity. They may be regarded as the two aspects or expressions under which God or substance is unfolded to man. Here a step is made beyond the limits of the Eleatic philosophy. The famous theorem of Spinoza, 'Omnis determinatio est negatio,' is already contained in the 'negation is relation' of Plato's Sophist. The grand description of the philosopher in Republic VI, as the spectator of all time and all existence, may be paralleled with another famous expression of Spinoza, 'Contemplatio rerum sub specie eternitatis.' According to Spinoza finite objects are unreal, for they are conditioned by what is alien to them, and by one another. Human beings are included in the number of them. Hence there is no reality in human action and no place for right and wrong. Individuality is accident. The boasted freedom of the will is only a consciousness of necessity. Truth, he says, is the direction of the reason towards the infinite, in which all things repose; and herein lies the secret of man's well-being. In the exaltation of the reason or intellect, in the denial of the voluntariness of evil (Timaeus; Laws) Spinoza approaches nearer to Plato than in his conception of an infinite substance. As Socrates said that virtue is knowledge, so Spinoza would have maintained that knowledge alone is good, and what contributes to knowledge useful. Both are equally far from any real experience or observation of nature. And the same difficulty is found in both when we seek to apply their ideas to life and practice. There is a gulf fixed between the infinite substance and finite objects or individuals of Spinoza, just as there is between the ideas of Plato and the world of sense.

Removed from Spinoza by less than a generation is the philosopher Leibnitz, who after deepening and intensifying the opposition between mind and matter, reunites them by his preconcerted harmony (compare again Phaedrus). To him all the particles of matter are living beings which reflect on one another, and in the least of them the whole is contained. Here we catch a reminiscence both of the omoiomere, or similar particles of Anaxagoras, and of the world-animal of the Timaeus.

In Bacon and Locke we have another development in which the mind of man is supposed to receive knowledge by a new method and to work by observation and experience. But we may remark that it is the idea of experience, rather than experience itself, with which the mind is filled. It is a symbol of knowledge rather than the reality which is vouchsafed to us. The Organon of Bacon is not much nearer to actual facts than the Organon of Aristotle or the Platonic idea of good. Many of the old rags and ribbons which defaced the garment of philosophy have been stripped off, but some of them still adhere. A crude conception of the ideas of Plato survives in the 'forms' of Bacon. And on the other hand, there are many passages of Plato in which the importance of the investigation of facts is as much insisted upon as by Bacon. Both are almost equally superior to the illusions of language, and are constantly crying out against them, as against other idols.

Locke cannot be truly regarded as the author of sensationalism any more than of idealism. His system is based upon experience, but with him experience includes reflection as well as sense. His analysis and construction of ideas has no foundation in fact; it is only the dialectic of the mind 'talking to herself.' The philosophy of Berkeley is but the transposition of two words. For objects of sense he would substitute sensations. He imagines himself to have changed the relation of the human mind towards God and nature; they remain the same as before, though he has drawn the imaginary line by which they are divided at a different point. He has annihilated the outward world, but it instantly reappears governed by the same laws and described under the same names.

A like remark applies to David Hume, of whose philosophy the central principle is the denial of the relation of cause and effect. He would deprive men of a familiar term which they can ill afford to lose; but he seems not to have observed that this alteration is merely verbal and does not in any degree affect the nature of things. Still less did he remark that he was arguing from the necessary imperfection of language against the most certain facts. And here, again, we may find a parallel with the ancients. He goes beyond facts in his scepticism, as they did in their idealism. Like the ancient Sophists, he relegates the more important principles of ethics to custom and probability. But crude and unmeaning as this philosophy is, it exercised a great influence on his successors, not unlike that which Locke exercised upon Berkeley and Berkeley upon Hume himself. All three were both sceptical and ideal in almost equal degrees. Neither they nor their predecessors had any true conception of language or of the history of philosophy. Hume's paradox has been forgotten by the world, and did not any more than the scepticism of the ancients require to be seriously refuted. Like some other philosophical paradoxes, it would have been better left to die out. It certainly could not be refuted by a philosophy such as Kant's, in which, no less than in the previously mentioned systems, the history of the human mind and the nature of language are almost wholly ignored, and the certainty of objective knowledge is transferred to the subject; while absolute truth is reduced to a figment, more abstract and narrow than Plato's ideas, of 'thing in itself,' to which, if we reason strictly, no predicate can be applied.

The question which Plato has raised respecting the origin and nature of ideas belongs to the infancy of philosophy; in modern times it would no longer be asked. Their origin is only their history, so far as we know it; there can be no other. We may trace them in language, in philosophy, in mythology, in poetry, but we cannot argue a priori about them. We may attempt to shake them off, but they are always returning, and in every sphere of science and human action are tending to go beyond facts. They are thought to be innate, because they have been familiar to us all our lives, and we can no longer dismiss them from our mind. Many of them express relations of terms to which nothing exactly or nothing at all in rerum natura corresponds. We are not such free agents in the use of them as we sometimes imagine. Fixed ideas have taken the most complete possession of some thinkers who have been most determined to renounce them, and have been vehemently affirmed when they could be least explained and were incapable of proof. The world has often been led away by a word to which no distinct meaning could be attached. Abstractions such as 'authority,' 'equality,' 'utility,' 'liberty,' 'pleasure,' 'experience,' 'consciousness,' 'chance,' 'substance,' 'matter,' 'atom,' and a heap of other metaphysical and theological terms, are the source of quite as much error and illusion and have as little relation to actual facts as the ideas of Plato. Few students of theology or philosophy have sufficiently reflected how quickly the bloom of a philosophy passes away; or how hard it is for one age to understand the writings of another; or how nice a judgment is required of those who are seeking to express the philosophy of one age in the terms of another. The 'eternal truths' of which metaphysicians speak have hardly ever lasted more than a generation. In our own day schools or systems of philosophy which have once been famous have died before the founders of them. We are still, as in Plato's age, groping about for a new method more comprehensive than any of those which now prevail; and also more permanent. And we seem to see at a distance the promise of such a method, which can hardly be any other than the method of idealized experience, having roots which strike far down into the history of philosophy. It is a method which does not divorce the present from the past, or the part from the whole, or the abstract from the concrete, or theory from fact, or the divine from the human, or one science from another, but labours to connect them. Along such a road we have proceeded a few steps, sufficient, perhaps, to make us reflect on the want of method which prevails in our own day. In another age, all the branches of knowledge, whether relating to God or man or nature, will become the knowledge of 'the revelation of a single science' (Symp.), and all things, like the stars in heaven, will shed their light upon one another.

MENO

PERSONS OF THE DIALOGUE:

Meno,
Socrates,
A Slave of Meno (Boy),
Anytus.

MENO:

Can you tell me, Socrates, whether virtue is acquired by teaching or by practice; or if neither by teaching nor by practice, then whether it comes to man by nature, or in what other way?

SOCRATES:

O Meno, there was a time when the Thessalians were famous among the other Hellenes only for their riches and their riding; but now, if I am not mistaken, they are equally famous for their wisdom, especially at Larisa, which is the native city of your friend Aristippus. And this is Gorgias' doing; for when he came there, the flower of the Aleuadae, among them your admirer Aristippus, and the other chiefs of the Thessalians, fell in love with his wisdom. And he has taught you the habit of answering questions in a

grand and bold style, which becomes those who
know, and is the style in which he himself answers all comers; and any Hellene who likes may
ask him anything. How different is our lot! my
dear Meno. Here at Athens there is a dearth of
the commodity, and all wisdom seems to have
emigrated from us to you. I am certain that if
you were to ask any Athenian whether virtue
was natural or acquired, he would laugh in your
face, and say: 'Stranger, you have far too good
an opinion of me, if you think that I can answer
your question. For I literally do not know what
virtue is, and much less whether it is acquired
by teaching or not.' And I myself, Meno, living as
I do in this region of poverty, am as poor as the
rest of the world; and I confess with shame that
I know literally nothing about virtue; and when
I do not know the 'quid' of anything how can I
know the 'quale'? How, if I knew nothing at all of
Meno, could I tell if he was fair, or the opposite
of fair; rich and noble, or the reverse of rich and
noble? Do you think that I could?

MENO:

No, indeed. But are you in earnest, Socrates, in
saying that you do not know what virtue is? And
am I to carry back this report of you to Thessaly?

SOCRATES:

Not only that, my dear boy, but you may say further that I have never known of any one else who
did, in my judgment.

MENO:

Then you have never met Gorgias when he was
at Athens?

SOCRATES:

Yes, I have.

MENO:

And did you not think that he knew?

SOCRATES:

I have not a good memory, Meno, and therefore I cannot now tell what I thought of him at the time. And I dare say that he did know, and that you know what he said: please, therefore, to remind me of what he said; or, if you would rather, tell me your own view; for I suspect that you and he think much alike.

MENO:

Very true.

SOCRATES:

Then as he is not here, never mind him, and do you tell me: By the gods, Meno, be generous, and tell me what you say that virtue is; for I shall be truly delighted to find that I have been mistaken, and that you and Gorgias do really have this knowledge; although I have been just saying that I have never found anybody who had.

MENO:

There will be no difficulty, Socrates, in answering your question. Let us take first the virtue of a man—he should know how to administer the state, and in the administration of it to benefit his friends and harm his enemies; and he must also be careful not to suffer harm himself. A woman's virtue, if you wish to know about that, may also be easily described: her duty is to order her house, and keep what is indoors, and obey her husband. Every age, every condition of life, young or old, male or female, bond or free, has a different virtue: there are virtues numberless, and no lack of definitions of them; for virtue is relative to the actions and ages of each of us in all that we do. And the same may be said of vice, Socrates (Compare Arist. Pol.).

SOCRATES:

How fortunate I am, Meno! When I ask you for one virtue, you present me with a swarm of them (Compare Theaet.), which are in your keeping. Suppose that I carry on the figure of the swarm, and ask of you, What is the nature of the bee? and you answer that there are many kinds of bees, and I reply: But do bees differ as bees, because there are many and different kinds of them; or are they not rather to be distinguished by some other quality, as for example beauty, size, or shape? How would you answer me?

MENO:

I should answer that bees do not differ from one another, as bees.

SOCRATES:

And if I went on to say: That is what I desire to know, Meno; tell me what is the quality in which they do not differ, but are all alike;—would you be able to answer?

MENO:

I should.

SOCRATES:

And so of the virtues, however many and different they may be, they have all a common nature which makes them virtues; and on this he who would answer the question, 'What is virtue?' would do well to have his eye fixed: Do you understand?

MENO:

I am beginning to understand; but I do not as yet take hold of the question as I could wish.

SOCRATES:

When you say, Meno, that there is one virtue of a man, another of a woman, another of a child, and so on, does this apply only to virtue, or would you say the same of health, and size, and strength? Or is the nature of health always the same, whether in man or woman?

MENO:

I should say that health is the same, both in man and woman.

SOCRATES:

And is not this true of size and strength? If a woman is strong, she will be strong by reason of the same form and of the same strength subsisting in her which there is in the man. I mean to say that strength, as strength, whether of man or woman, is the same. Is there any difference?

MENO:

I think not.

SOCRATES:

And will not virtue, as virtue, be the same, whether in a child or in a grown-up person, in a woman or in a man?

MENO:

I cannot help feeling, Socrates, that this case is different from the others.

SOCRATES:

But why? Were you not saying that the virtue of a man was to order a state, and the virtue of a woman was to order a house?

MENO:

I did say so.

SOCRATES:

And can either house or state or anything be well ordered without temperance and without justice?

MENO:

Certainly not.

SOCRATES:

Then they who order a state or a house temperately or justly order them with temperance and justice?

MENO:

Certainly.

SOCRATES:

Then both men and women, if they are to be good men and women, must have the same virtues of temperance and justice?

MENO:

True.

SOCRATES:

And can either a young man or an elder one be good, if they are intemperate and unjust?

MENO:

They cannot.

SOCRATES:

They must be temperate and just?

MENO:

Yes.

SOCRATES:

Then all men are good in the same way, and by participation in the same virtues?

MENO:

Such is the inference.

SOCRATES:

And they surely would not have been good in the same way, unless their virtue had been the same?

MENO:

They would not.

SOCRATES:

Then now that the sameness of all virtue has been proven, try and remember what you and Gorgias say that virtue is.

MENO:

Will you have one definition of them all?

SOCRATES:

That is what I am seeking.

MENO:

If you want to have one definition of them all, I know not what to say, but that virtue is the power of governing mankind.

SOCRATES:

And does this definition of virtue include all virtue? Is virtue the same in a child and in a slave, Meno? Can the child govern his father, or the slave his master; and would he who governed be any longer a slave?

MENO:

I think not, Socrates.

SOCRATES:

No, indeed; there would be small reason in that. Yet once more, fair friend; according to you, virtue is 'the power of governing;' but do you not add 'justly and not unjustly'?

MENO:

Yes, Socrates; I agree there; for justice is virtue.

SOCRATES:

Would you say 'virtue,' Meno, or 'a virtue'?

MENO:

What do you mean?

SOCRATES:

I mean as I might say about anything; that a round, for example, is 'a figure' and not simply 'figure,' and I should adopt this mode of speaking, because there are other figures.

MENO:

Quite right; and that is just what I am saying about virtue—that there are other virtues as well as justice.

SOCRATES:

What are they? tell me the names of them, as I would tell you the names of the other figures if you asked me.

MENO:

Courage and temperance and wisdom and magnanimity are virtues; and there are many others.

SOCRATES:

Yes, Meno; and again we are in the same case: in searching after one virtue we have found many, though not in the same way as before; but we have been unable to find the common virtue which runs through them all.

MENO:

Why, Socrates, even now I am not able to follow you in the attempt to get at one common notion of virtue as of other things.

SOCRATES:

No wonder; but I will try to get nearer if I can, for you know that all things have a common notion. Suppose now that some one asked you the question which I asked before: Meno, he would say, what is figure? And if you answered 'roundness,' he would reply to you, in my way of speaking, by asking whether you would say that roundness is 'figure' or 'a figure;' and you would answer 'a figure.'

MENO:

Certainly.

SOCRATES:

And for this reason—that there are other figures?

MENO:

Yes.

SOCRATES:

And if he proceeded to ask, What other figures are there? you would have told him.

MENO:

I should.

SOCRATES:

And if he similarly asked what colour is, and you answered whiteness, and the questioner rejoined, Would you say that whiteness is colour or a colour? you would reply, A colour, because there are other colours as well.

MENO:

I should.

SOCRATES:

And if he had said, Tell me what they are?—you would have told him of other colours which are colours just as much as whiteness.

MENO:

Yes.

SOCRATES:

And suppose that he were to pursue the matter in my way, he would say: Ever and anon we are landed in particulars, but this is not what I want; tell me then, since you call them by a common name, and say that they are all figures, even when opposed to one another, what is that common nature which you designate as figure—which contains straight as well as round, and is no more one than the other—that would be your mode of speaking?

MENO:

Yes.

SOCRATES:

And in speaking thus, you do not mean to say that the round is round any more than straight, or the straight any more straight than round?

MENO:

Certainly not.

SOCRATES:

You only assert that the round figure is not more a figure than the straight, or the straight than the round?

MENO:

Very true.

SOCRATES:

To what then do we give the name of figure? Try and answer. Suppose that when a person asked you this question either about figure or colour, you were to reply, Man, I do not understand what you want, or know what you are saying; he would look rather astonished and say: Do you not understand that I am looking for the 'simile in multis'? And then he might put the question in another form: Meno, he might say, what is that 'simile in multis' which you call figure, and which includes not only round and straight figures, but all? Could you not answer that question, Meno? I wish that you would try; the attempt will be good practice with a view to the answer about virtue.

MENO:

I would rather that you should answer, Socrates.

SOCRATES:

Shall I indulge you?

MENO:

By all means.

SOCRATES:

And then you will tell me about virtue?

MENO:

I will.

SOCRATES:

Then I must do my best, for there is a prize to be won.

MENO:

Certainly.

SOCRATES:

Well, I will try and explain to you what figure is. What do you say to this answer?—Figure is the only thing which always follows colour. Will you be satisfied with it, as I am sure that I should be, if you would let me have a similar definition of virtue?

MENO:

But, Socrates, it is such a simple answer.

SOCRATES:

Why simple?

MENO:

Because, according to you, figure is that which always follows colour.

(SOCRATES:

Granted.)

MENO:

But if a person were to say that he does not know what colour is, any more than what figure is— what sort of answer would you have given him?

SOCRATES:

I should have told him the truth. And if he were a philosopher of the eristic and antagonistic sort, I should say to him: You have my answer, and if I am wrong, your business is to take up the argument and refute me. But if we were friends, and were talking as you and I are now, I should reply in a milder strain and more in the dialectician's vein; that is to say, I should not only speak the truth, but I should make use of premisses which the person interrogated would be willing to admit. And this is the way in which I shall endeavour to approach you. You will acknowledge, will you not, that there is such a thing as an end, or termination, or extremity?—all which words I use in the same sense, although I am aware that Prodicus might draw distinctions about them: but still you, I am sure, would speak of a thing as ended or terminated—that is all which I am saying—not anything very difficult.

MENO:

Yes, I should; and I believe that I understand your meaning.

SOCRATES:

And you would speak of a surface and also of a solid, as for example in geometry.

MENO:

Yes.

SOCRATES:

Well then, you are now in a condition to understand my definition of figure. I define figure to be that in which the solid ends; or, more concisely, the limit of solid.

MENO:

And now, Socrates, what is colour?

SOCRATES:

You are outrageous, Meno, in thus plaguing a poor old man to give you an answer, when you will not take the trouble of remembering what is Gorgias' definition of virtue.

MENO:

When you have told me what I ask, I will tell you, Socrates.

SOCRATES:

A man who was blindfolded has only to hear you talking, and he would know that you are a fair creature and have still many lovers.

MENO:

Why do you think so?

SOCRATES:

Why, because you always speak in imperatives: like all beauties when they are in their prime, you are tyrannical; and also, as I suspect, you have found out that I have weakness for the fair, and therefore to humour you I must answer.

MENO:

Please do.

SOCRATES:

Would you like me to answer you after the manner of Gorgias, which is familiar to you?

MENO:

I should like nothing better.

SOCRATES:

Do not he and you and Empedocles say that there are certain effluences of existence?

MENO:

Certainly.

SOCRATES:

And passages into which and through which the effluences pass?

MENO:

Exactly.

SOCRATES:

And some of the effluences fit into the passages, and some of them are too small or too large?

MENO:

True.

SOCRATES:

And there is such a thing as sight?

MENO:

Yes.

SOCRATES:

And now, as Pindar says, 'read my mean-ing:'— colour is an effluence of form, commensurate with sight, and palpable to sense.

MENO:

That, Socrates, appears to me to be an admirable answer.

SOCRATES:

Why, yes, because it happens to be one which you have been in the habit of hearing: and your wit will have discovered, I suspect, that you may explain in the same way the nature of sound and smell, and of many other similar phenomena.

MENO:

Quite true.

SOCRATES:

The answer, Meno, was in the orthodox solemn vein, and therefore was more acceptable to you than the other answer about figure.

MENO:

Yes.

SOCRATES:

And yet, O son of Alexidemus, I cannot help thinking that the other was the better; and I am sure that you would be of the same opinion, if you would only stay and be initiated, and were not compelled, as you said yesterday, to go away before the mysteries.

MENO:

But I will stay, Socrates, if you will give me many such answers.

SOCRATES:

Well then, for my own sake as well as for yours, I will do my very best; but I am afraid that I shall not be able to give you very many as good: and now, in your turn, you are to fulfil your promise, and tell me what virtue is in the universal; and do not make a singular into a plural, as the facetious say of those who break a thing, but deliver virtue to me whole and sound, and not broken into a number of pieces: I have given you the pattern.

MENO:

Well then, Socrates, virtue, as I take it, is when he, who desires the honourable, is able to provide it for himself; so the poet says, and I say too—

'Virtue is the desire of things honourable and the power of attaining them.'

SOCRATES:

And does he who desires the honourable also desire the good?

MENO:

Certainly.

SOCRATES:

Then are there some who desire the evil and others who desire the good? Do not all men, my dear sir, desire good?

MENO:

I think not.

SOCRATES:

There are some who desire evil?

MENO:

Yes.

SOCRATES:

Do you mean that they think the evils which they desire, to be good; or do they know that they are evil and yet desire them?

MENO:

Both, I think.

SOCRATES:

And do you really imagine, Meno, that a man knows evils to be evils and desires them notwithstanding?

MENO:

Certainly I do.

SOCRATES:

And desire is of possession?

MENO:

Yes, of possession.

SOCRATES:

And does he think that the evils will do good to him who possesses them, or does he know that they will do him harm?

MENO:

There are some who think that the evils will do them good, and others who know that they will do them harm.

SOCRATES:

And, in your opinion, do those who think that they will do them good know that they are evils?

MENO:

Certainly not.

SOCRATES:

Is it not obvious that those who are ignorant of their nature do not desire them; but they desire what they suppose to be goods although they are really evils; and if they are mistaken and suppose the evils to be goods they really desire goods?

MENO:

Yes, in that case.

SOCRATES:

Well, and do those who, as you say, desire evils, and think that evils are hurtful to the possessor of them, know that they will be hurt by them?

MENO:

They must know it.

SOCRATES:

And must they not suppose that those who are hurt are miserable in proportion to the hurt which is inflicted upon them?

MENO:

How can it be otherwise?

SOCRATES:

But are not the miserable ill-fated?

MENO:

Yes, indeed.

SOCRATES:

And does any one desire to be miserable and ill-fated?

MENO:

I should say not, Socrates.

SOCRATES:

But if there is no one who desires to be miserable, there is no one, Meno, who desires evil; for what is misery but the desire and possession of evil?

MENO:

That appears to be the truth, Socrates, and I admit that nobody desires evil.

SOCRATES:

And yet, were you not saying just now that virtue is the desire and power of attaining good?

MENO:

Yes, I did say so.

SOCRATES:

But if this be affirmed, then the desire of good is common to all, and one man is no better than another in that respect?

MENO:

True.

SOCRATES:

And if one man is not better than another in

53

desiring good, he must be better in the power of attaining it?

MENO:

Exactly.

SOCRATES:

Then, according to your definition, virtue would appear to be the power of attaining good?

MENO:

I entirely approve, Socrates, of the manner in which you now view this matter.

SOCRATES:

Then let us see whether what you say is true from another point of view; for very likely you may be right:—You affirm virtue to be the power of attaining goods?

MENO:

Yes.

SOCRATES:

And the goods which you mean are such as health and wealth and the possession of gold and silver, and having office and honour in the state—those are what you would call goods?

MENO:

Yes, I should include all those.

SOCRATES:

Then, according to Meno, who is the hereditary friend of the great king, virtue is the power of getting silver and gold; and would you add that they must be gained piously, justly, or do you deem this to be of no consequence? And is any mode of acquisition, even if unjust and dishonest, equally to be deemed virtue?

MENO:

Not virtue, Socrates, but vice.

SOCRATES:

Then justice or temperance or holiness, or some other part of virtue, as would appear, must accompany the acquisition, and without them the mere acquisition of good will not be virtue.

MENO:

Why, how can there be virtue without these?

SOCRATES:

And the non-acquisition of gold and silver in a dishonest manner for oneself or another, or in other words the want of them, may be equally virtue?

MENO:

True.

SOCRATES:

Then the acquisition of such goods is no more virtue than the non-acquisition and want of them, but whatever is accompanied by justice or honesty is virtue, and whatever is devoid of justice is vice.

MENO:

It cannot be otherwise, in my judgment.

SOCRATES:

And were we not saying just now that justice, temperance, and the like, were each of them a part of virtue?

MENO:

Yes.

SOCRATES:

And so, Meno, this is the way in which you mock me.

MENO:

Why do you say that, Socrates?

SOCRATES:

Why, because I asked you to deliver virtue into my hands whole and unbroken, and I gave you a pattern according to which you were to frame your answer; and you have forgotten already, and tell me that virtue is the power of attaining good justly, or with justice; and justice you acknowledge to be a part of virtue.

MENO:

Yes.

SOCRATES:

Then it follows from your own admissions, that virtue is doing what you do with a part of virtue; for justice and the like are said by you to be parts of virtue.

MENO:

What of that?

SOCRATES:

What of that! Why, did not I ask you to tell me the nature of virtue as a whole? And you are very far from telling me this; but declare every action to be virtue which is done with a part of virtue; as though you had told me and I must already know the whole of virtue, and this too when frittered away into little pieces. And, therefore, my dear Meno, I fear that I must begin again and repeat the same question: What is virtue? for otherwise, I can only say, that every action done with a part of virtue is virtue; what else is the meaning of saying that every action done with justice is virtue? Ought I not to ask the question over again; for can any one who does not know virtue know a part of virtue?

MENO:

No; I do not say that he can.

SOCRATES:

Do you remember how, in the example of figure, we rejected any answer given in terms which were as yet unexplained or unadmitted?

MENO:

Yes, Socrates; and we were quite right in doing so.

SOCRATES:

But then, my friend, do not suppose that we can explain to any one the nature of virtue as a whole through some unexplained portion of virtue, or anything at all in that fashion; we should only have to ask over again the old question, What is virtue? Am I not right?

MENO:

I believe that you are.

SOCRATES:

Then begin again, and answer me, What, according to you and your friend Gorgias, is the definition of virtue?

MENO:

O Socrates, I used to be told, before I knew you, that you were always doubting yourself and making others doubt; and now you are casting your spells over me, and I am simply getting bewitched and enchanted, and am at my wits' end. And if I may venture to make a jest upon you,

you seem to me both in your appearance and in your power over others to be very like the flat torpedo fish, who torpifies those who come near him and touch him, as you have now torpified me, I think. For my soul and my tongue are really torpid, and I do not know how to answer you; and though I have been delivered of an infinite variety of speeches about virtue before now, and to many persons—and very good ones they were, as I thought—at this moment I cannot even say what virtue is. And I think that you are very wise in not voyaging and going away from home, for if you did in other places as you do in Athens, you would be cast into prison as a magician.

SOCRATES:

You are a rogue, Meno, and had all but caught me.

MENO:

What do you mean, Socrates?

SOCRATES:

I can tell why you made a simile about me.

MENO:

Why?

SOCRATES:

In order that I might make another simile about you. For I know that all pretty young gentlemen like to have pretty similes made about them—as well they may—but I shall not return the compliment. As to my being a torpedo, if the torpedo is torpid as well as the cause of torpidity in others, then indeed I am a torpedo, but not otherwise; for I perplex others, not because I am clear, but because I am utterly perplexed myself. And now I know not what virtue is, and you seem to be in the same case, although you did once perhaps know before you touched me. However, I have no objection to join with you in the enquiry.

MENO:

And how will you enquire, Socrates, into that which you do not know? What will you put forth as the subject of enquiry? And if you find what you want, how will you ever know that this is the thing which you did not know?

SOCRATES:

I know, Meno, what you mean; but just see what a tiresome dispute you are introducing. You argue that a man cannot enquire either about that which he knows, or about that which he does not know; for if he knows, he has no need to enquire; and if not, he cannot; for he does not know the very subject about which he is to enquire (Compare Aristot. Post. Anal.).

MENO:

Well, Socrates, and is not the argument sound?

SOCRATES:

I think not.

MENO:

Why not?

SOCRATES:

I will tell you why: I have heard from certain wise men and women who spoke of things divine that—

MENO:

What did they say?

SOCRATES:

They spoke of a glorious truth, as I conceive.

MENO:

What was it? and who were they?

SOCRATES:

Some of them were priests and priestesses, who had studied how they might be able to give a reason of their profession: there have been poets also, who spoke of these things by inspiration, like Pindar, and many others who were inspired. And they say—mark, now, and see whether their words are true—they say that the soul of man is immortal, and at one time has an end, which is termed dying, and at another time is born again, but is never destroyed. And the moral is, that a man ought to live always in perfect holiness. 'For in the ninth year Persephone sends the souls of those from whom she has received the penalty of ancient crime back again from beneath into the light of the sun above, and these are they who become noble kings and mighty men and great in wisdom and are called saintly heroes in after ages.' The soul, then, as being immortal, and having been born again many times, and having seen all things that exist, whether in this world or in the world below, has knowledge of them all; and it is no wonder that she should be able to call to remembrance all that she ever knew about virtue, and about everything; for as all nature is akin, and the soul has learned all things; there is no difficulty in her eliciting or as men say learning, out of a single recollection all the rest, if a man is strenuous and does not faint; for all enquiry and all learning is but recollection. And therefore we ought not to listen to this sophistical argument about the impossibility of enquiry: for it will make us idle; and is sweet only to the sluggard; but the other saying will make us active and inquisitive. In that confiding, I will gladly enquire with you into the nature of virtue.

MENO:

Yes, Socrates; but what do you mean by say-ing that we do not learn, and that what we call learning is only a process of recollection? Can you teach me how this is?

SOCRATES:

I told you, Meno, just now that you were a rogue, and now you ask whether I can teach you, when I am saying that there is no teaching, but only recollection; and thus you imagine that you will involve me in a contradiction.

MENO:

Indeed, Socrates, I protest that I had no such intention. I only asked the question from habit; but if you can prove to me that what you say is true, I wish that you would.

SOCRATES:

It will be no easy matter, but I will try to please you to the utmost of my power. Suppose that you call one of your numerous attendants, that I may demonstrate on him.

MENO:

Certainly. Come hither, boy.

SOCRATES:

He is Greek, and speaks Greek, does he not?

MENO:

Yes, indeed; he was born in the house.

SOCRATES:

Attend now to the questions which I ask him, and observe whether he learns of me or only remembers.

MENO:

I will.

SOCRATES:

Tell me, boy, do you know that a figure like this is a square?

BOY:

I do.

SOCRATES:

And you know that a square figure has these four lines equal?

BOY:

Certainly.

SOCRATES:

And these lines which I have drawn through the middle of the square are also equal?

BOY:

Yes.

SOCRATES:

A square may be of any size?

BOY:

Certainly.

SOCRATES:

And if one side of the figure be of two feet, and the other side be of two feet, how much will the whole be? Let me explain: if in one direction the space was of two feet, and in the other direction of one foot, the whole would be of two feet taken once?

BOY:

Yes.

SOCRATES:

But since this side is also of two feet, there are twice two feet?

BOY:

There are.

SOCRATES:

Then the square is of twice two feet?

BOY:

Yes.

SOCRATES:

And how many are twice two feet? count and tell me.

BOY:

Four, Socrates.

SOCRATES:

And might there not be another square twice as large as this, and having like this the lines equal?

BOY:

Yes.

SOCRATES:

And of how many feet will that be?

BOY:

Of eight feet.

SOCRATES:

And now try and tell me the length of the line which forms the side of that double square: this is two feet—what will that be?

BOY:

Clearly, Socrates, it will be double.

SOCRATES:

Do you observe, Meno, that I am not teaching the boy anything, but only asking him questions; and now he fancies that he knows how long a line is necessary in order to produce a figure of eight square feet; does he not?

MENO:

Yes.

SOCRATES:

And does he really know?

MENO:

Certainly not.

SOCRATES:

He only guesses that because the square is double, the line is double.

MENO:

True.

SOCRATES:

Observe him while he recalls the steps in regular order. (To the Boy:) Tell me, boy, do you assert that a double space comes from a double line? Remember that I am not speaking of an oblong, but of a figure equal every way, and twice the size of this—that is to say of eight feet; and I want to know whether you still say that a double square comes from double line?

BOY:

Yes.

SOCRATES:

But does not this line become doubled if we add another such line here?

BOY:

Certainly.

SOCRATES:

And four such lines will make a space containing eight feet?

BOY:

Yes.

SOCRATES:

Let us describe such a figure: Would you not say that this is the figure of eight feet?

BOY:

Yes.

SOCRATES:

And are there not these four divisions in the figure, each of which is equal to the figure of four feet?

BOY:

True.

SOCRATES:

And is not that four times four?

BOY:

Certainly.

SOCRATES:

And four times is not double?

BOY:

No, indeed.

SOCRATES:

But how much?

BOY:

Four times as much.

SOCRATES:

Therefore the double line, boy, has given a space, not twice, but four times as much.

BOY:

True.

SOCRATES:

Four times four are sixteen—are they not?

BOY:

Yes.

SOCRATES:

What line would give you a space of eight feet, as this gives one of sixteen feet;—do you see?

BOY:

Yes.

SOCRATES:

And the space of four feet is made from this half line?

BOY:

Yes.

SOCRATES:

Good; and is not a space of eight feet twice the size of this, and half the size of the other?

BOY:

Certainly.

SOCRATES:

Such a space, then, will be made out of a line greater than this one, and less than that one?

BOY:

Yes; I think so.

SOCRATES:

Very good; I like to hear you say what you think. And now tell me, is not this a line of two feet and that of four?

BOY:

Yes.

SOCRATES:

Then the line which forms the side of eight feet ought to be more than this line of two feet, and less than the other of four feet?

BOY:

It ought.

SOCRATES:

Try and see if you can tell me how much it will be.

BOY:

Three feet.

SOCRATES:

Then if we add a half to this line of two, that will be the line of three. Here are two and there is one; and on the other side, here are two also and there is one: and that makes the figure of which you speak?

BOY:

Yes.

SOCRATES:

But if there are three feet this way and three feet that way, the whole space will be three times three feet?

BOY:

That is evident.

SOCRATES:

And how much are three times three feet?

BOY:

Nine.

SOCRATES:

And how much is the double of four?

BOY:

Eight.

SOCRATES:

Then the figure of eight is not made out of a line of three?

BOY:

No.

SOCRATES:

But from what line?—tell me exactly; and if you would rather not reckon, try and show me the line.

BOY:

Indeed, Socrates, I do not know.

SOCRATES:

Do you see, Meno, what advances he has made in his power of recollection? He did not know at first, and he does not know now, what is the side of a figure of eight feet: but then he thought that he knew, and answered confidently as if he knew, and had no difficulty; now he has a difficulty, and neither knows nor fancies that he knows.

MENO:

True.

SOCRATES:

Is he not better off in knowing his ignorance?

MENO:

I think that he is.

SOCRATES:

If we have made him doubt, and given him the 'torpedo's shock,' have we done him any harm?

MENO:

I think not.

SOCRATES:

We have certainly, as would seem, assisted him in some degree to the discovery of the truth; and now he will wish to remedy his ignorance, but then he would have been ready to tell all the world again and again that the double space should have a double side.

MENO:

True.

SOCRATES:

But do you suppose that he would ever have enquired into or learned what he fancied that he knew, though he was really ignorant of it, until he had fallen into perplexity under the idea that he did not know, and had desired to know?

MENO:

I think not, Socrates.

SOCRATES:

Then he was the better for the torpedo's touch?

MENO:

I think so.

SOCRATES:

Mark now the farther development. I shall only ask him, and not teach him, and he shall share the enquiry with me: and do you watch and see if you find me telling or explaining anything to him, instead of eliciting his opinion. Tell me, boy, is not this a square of four feet which I have drawn?

BOY:

Yes.

SOCRATES:

And now I add another square equal to the former one?

BOY:

Yes.

SOCRATES:

And a third, which is equal to either of them?

BOY:

Yes.

SOCRATES:

Suppose that we fill up the vacant corner?

BOY:

Very good.

SOCRATES:

Here, then, there are four equal spaces?

BOY:

Yes.

SOCRATES:

And how many times larger is this space than this other?

BOY:

Four times.

SOCRATES:

But it ought to have been twice only, as you will remember.

BOY:

True.

SOCRATES:

And does not this line, reaching from corner to corner, bisect each of these spaces?

BOY:

Yes.

SOCRATES:

And are there not here four equal lines which contain this space?

BOY:

There are.

SOCRATES:

Look and see how much this space is.

BOY:

I do not understand.

SOCRATES:

Has not each interior line cut off half of the four spaces?

BOY:

Yes.

SOCRATES:

And how many spaces are there in this section?

BOY:

Four.

SOCRATES:

And how many in this?

BOY:

Two.

SOCRATES:

And four is how many times two?

BOY:

Twice.

SOCRATES:

And this space is of how many feet?

BOY:

Of eight feet.

SOCRATES:

And from what line do you get this figure?

BOY:

From this.

SOCRATES:

That is, from the line which extends from corner to corner of the figure of four feet?

BOY:

Yes.

SOCRATES:

And that is the line which the learned call the diagonal. And if this is the proper name, then

you, Meno's slave, are prepared to affirm that
the double space is the square of the diagonal?

BOY:

Certainly, Socrates.

SOCRATES:

What do you say of him, Meno? Were not all
these answers given out of his own head?

MENO:

Yes, they were all his own.

SOCRATES:

And yet, as we were just now saying, he did not
know?

MENO:

True.

SOCRATES:

But still he had in him those notions of his—had
he not?

MENO:

Yes.

SOCRATES:

Then he who does not know may still have true
notions of that which he does not know?

MENO:

He has.

SOCRATES:

And at present these notions have just been
stirred up in him, as in a dream; but if he
were frequently asked the same questions, in
different forms, he would know as well as any
one at last?

MENO:

I dare say.

SOCRATES:

Without any one teaching him he will recover his knowledge for himself, if he is only asked questions?

MENO:

Yes.

SOCRATES:

And this spontaneous recovery of knowledge in him is recollection?

MENO:

True.

SOCRATES:

And this knowledge which he now has must he not either have acquired or always possessed?

MENO:

Yes.

SOCRATES:

But if he always possessed this knowledge he would always have known; or if he has acquired the knowledge he could not have acquired it in this life, unless he has been taught geometry; for he may be made to do the same with all geometry and every other branch of knowledge. Now, has any one ever taught him all this? You must know about him, if, as you say, he was born and bred in your house.

MENO:

And I am certain that no one ever did teach him.

SOCRATES:

And yet he has the knowledge?

MENO:

The fact, Socrates, is undeniable.

SOCRATES:

But if he did not acquire the knowledge in this life, then he must have had and learned it at some other time?

MENO:

Clearly he must.

SOCRATES:

Which must have been the time when he was not a man?

MENO:

Yes.

SOCRATES:

And if there have been always true thoughts in him, both at the time when he was and was not a man, which only need to be awakened into knowledge by putting questions to him, his soul must have always possessed this knowledge, for he always either was or was not a man?

MENO:

Obviously.

SOCRATES:

And if the truth of all things always existed in the soul, then the soul is immortal. Wherefore be of good cheer, and try to recollect what you do not know, or rather what you do not remember.

MENO:

I feel, somehow, that I like what you are saying.

SOCRATES:

And I, Meno, like what I am saying. Some things I have said of which I am not altogether confident. But that we shall be better and braver and less helpless if we think that we ought to enquire, than we should have been if we indulged in the idle fancy that there was no knowing and no use in seeking to know what we do not know;—that is a theme upon which I am ready to fight, in word and deed, to the utmost of my power.

MENO:

There again, Socrates, your words seem to me excellent.

SOCRATES:

Then, as we are agreed that a man should enquire about that which he does not know, shall you and I make an effort to enquire together into the nature of virtue?

MENO:

By all means, Socrates. And yet I would much rather return to my original question, Whether in seeking to acquire virtue we should regard it as a thing to be taught, or as a gift of nature, or as coming to men in some other way?

SOCRATES:

Had I the command of you as well as of myself, Meno, I would not have enquired whether virtue is given by instruction or not, until we had first ascertained 'what it is.' But as you think only of controlling me who am your slave, and never of controlling yourself,—such being your notion of freedom, I must yield to you, for you are irresistible. And therefore I have now to enquire into the qualities of a thing of which I do not as yet know the nature. At any rate, will you condescend a little, and allow the question 'Whether virtue is given by instruction, or in any other way,' to be argued upon hypothesis? As the geometrician, when he is asked whether a certain triangle is capable being inscribed in a certain circle (Or, whether a certain area is capable of being inscribed as a triangle in a certain circle.), will reply: 'I cannot tell you as yet; but I will offer a hypothesis which may assist us in forming a conclusion: If the figure be such that when you have produced a given side of it (Or, when you apply it to the given line, i.e. the diameter of the circle (autou).), the given area of the triangle falls short by an area corresponding to the part produced (Or, similar to the area so applied.), then one consequence follows, and if this is impossible then some other; and therefore I wish to as-sume a hypothesis before I tell you whether this triangle is capable of being inscribed in the circle':—that is a geometrical hypothesis. And we too, as we know not the nature and qualities of virtue, must ask, whether virtue is or is not taught, under a hypothesis: as thus, if virtue is of such a class of mental goods, will it be taught or not? Let the first hypothesis be that virtue is or is not knowledge,—in that case will it be taught or not? or, as we were just now saying, 'remembered'? For there is no use in disputing about the name. But is virtue taught or not? or rather, does not every one see that knowledge alone is taught?

MENO:

I agree.

SOCRATES:

Then if virtue is knowledge, virtue will be taught?

MENO:

Certainly.

SOCRATES:

Then now we have made a quick end of this question: if virtue is of such a nature, it will be taught; and if not, not?

MENO:

Certainly.

SOCRATES:

The next question is, whether virtue is knowledge or of another species?

MENO:

Yes, that appears to be the question which comes next in order.

SOCRATES:

Do we not say that virtue is a good?—This is a hypothesis which is not set aside.

MENO:

Certainly.

SOCRATES:

Now, if there be any sort of good which is distinct from knowledge, virtue may be that good; but if knowledge embraces all good, then we shall be right in thinking that virtue is knowledge?

MENO:

True.

SOCRATES:

And virtue makes us good?

MENO:

Yes.

SOCRATES:

And if we are good, then we are profitable; for all good things are profitable?

MENO:

Yes.

SOCRATES:

Then virtue is profitable?

MENO:

That is the only inference.

SOCRATES:

Then now let us see what are the things which severally profit us. Health and strength, and beauty and wealth—these, and the like of these, we call profitable?

MENO:

True.

SOCRATES:

And yet these things may also sometimes do us harm: would you not think so?

MENO:

Yes.

SOCRATES:

And what is the guiding principle which makes them profitable or the reverse? Are they not profitable when they are rightly used, and hurtful when they are not rightly used?

MENO:

Certainly.

SOCRATES:

Next, let us consider the goods of the soul: they are temperance, justice, courage, quickness of apprehension, memory, magnanimity, and the like?

MENO:

Surely.

SOCRATES:

And such of these as are not knowledge, but of another sort, are sometimes profitable and sometimes hurtful; as, for example, courage wanting prudence, which is only a sort of confidence? When a man has no sense he is harmed by courage, but when he has sense he is profited?

MENO:

True.

SOCRATES:

And the same may be said of temperance and quickness of apprehension; whatever things are learned or done with sense are profitable, but when done without sense they are hurtful?

MENO:

Very true.

SOCRATES:

And in general, all that the soul attempts or endures, when under the guidance of wisdom, ends in happiness; but when she is under the guidance of folly, in the opposite?

MENO:

That appears to be true.

SOCRATES:

If then virtue is a quality of the soul, and is admitted to be profitable, it must be wisdom or prudence, since none of the things of the soul are either profitable or hurtful in themselves, but they are all made profitable or hurtful by the addition of wisdom or of folly; and therefore if virtue is profitable, virtue must be a sort of wisdom or prudence?

MENO:

I quite agree.

SOCRATES:

And the other goods, such as wealth and the like, of which we were just now saying that they are sometimes good and sometimes evil, do not they also become profitable or hurtful, accordingly as the soul guides and uses them rightly or wrongly; just as the things of the soul herself are benefited when under the guidance of wisdom and harmed by folly?

MENO:

True.

SOCRATES:

And the wise soul guides them rightly, and the foolish soul wrongly.

MENO:

Yes.

SOCRATES:

And is not this universally true of human nature? All other things hang upon the soul, and the things of the soul herself hang upon wisdom, if they are to be good; and so wisdom is inferred to be that which profits—and virtue, as we say, is profitable?

MENO:

Certainly.

SOCRATES:

And thus we arrive at the conclusion that virtue is either wholly or partly wisdom?

MENO:

I think that what you are saying, Socrates, is very true.

SOCRATES:

But if this is true, then the good are not by nature good?

MENO:

I think not.

SOCRATES:

If they had been, there would assuredly have been discerners of characters among us who would have known our future great men; and on their showing we should have adopted them, and when we had got them, we should have kept them in the citadel out of the way of harm, and set a stamp upon them far rather than upon a piece of gold, in order that no one might tamper with them; and when they grew up they would have been useful to the state?

MENO:

Yes, Socrates, that would have been the right way.

SOCRATES:

But if the good are not by nature good, are they made good by instruction?

MENO:

There appears to be no other alternative, Socrates. On the supposition that virtue is knowledge, there can be no doubt that virtue is taught.

SOCRATES:

Yes, indeed; but what if the supposition is erroneous?

MENO:

I certainly thought just now that we were right.

SOCRATES:

Yes, Meno; but a principle which has any soundness should stand firm not only just now, but always.

MENO:

Well; and why are you so slow of heart to believe that knowledge is virtue?

SOCRATES:

I will try and tell you why, Meno. I do not retract the assertion that if virtue is knowledge it may be taught; but I fear that I have some reason in doubting whether virtue is knowledge: for consider now and say whether virtue, and not only virtue but anything that is taught, must not have teachers and disciples?

MENO:

Surely.

SOCRATES:

And conversely, may not the art of which neither teachers nor disciples exist be assumed to be incapable of being taught?

MENO:

True; but do you think that there are no teachers of virtue?

SOCRATES:

I have certainly often enquired whether there were any, and taken great pains to find them, and have never succeeded; and many have assisted me in the search, and they were the persons whom I thought the most likely to know. Here at the moment when he is wanted we fortunately have sitting by us Anytus, the very person of whom we should make enquiry; to him then let us repair. In the first place, he is the son of a wealthy and wise father, Anthemion, who acquired his wealth, not by accident or gift, like Ismenias the Theban (who has recently made himself as rich as Polycrates), but by his own skill and industry, and who is a well-conditioned, modest man, not insolent, or overbearing, or annoying; moreover, this son of his has received a good education, as the Athenian people certainly appear to think, for they choose him to fill the highest offices. And these are the sort of men from whom you are likely to learn whether there are any teachers of virtue, and who they are. Please, Anytus, to help me and your friend Meno in answering our question, Who are the teachers? Consider the matter thus: If we wanted Meno to be a good physician, to whom should we send him? Should we not send him to the physicians?

ANYTUS:

Certainly.

SOCRATES:

Or if we wanted him to be a good cobbler, should we not send him to the cobblers?

ANYTUS:

Yes.

SOCRATES:

And so forth?

ANYTUS:

Yes.

SOCRATES:

Let me trouble you with one more question. When we say that we should be right in sending him to the physicians if we wanted him to be a physician, do we mean that we should be right in sending him to those who profess the art, rather than to those who do not, and to those who demand payment for teaching the art, and profess to teach it to any one who will come and learn? And if these were our reasons, should we not be right in sending him?

ANYTUS:

Yes.

SOCRATES:

And might not the same be said of flute-playing, and of the other arts? Would a man who wanted to make another a flute-player refuse to send him to those who profess to teach the art for money, and be plaguing other persons to give him instruction, who are not professed teachers and who never had a single disciple in that branch of knowledge which he wishes him to acquire— would not such conduct be the height of folly?

ANYTUS:

Yes, by Zeus, and of ignorance too.

SOCRATES:

Very good. And now you are in a position to advise with me about my friend Meno. He has been telling me, Anytus, that he desires to attain that kind of wisdom and virtue by which men order the state or the house, and honour their parents, and know when to receive and when to send away citizens and strangers, as a good man should. Now, to whom should he go in order that he may learn this virtue? Does not the previous argument imply clearly that we should send him to those who profess and avouch that they are the common teachers of all Hellas, and are ready to impart instruction to any one who likes, at a fixed price?

ANYTUS:

Whom do you mean, Socrates?

SOCRATES:

You surely know, do you not, Anytus, that these are the people whom mankind call Sophists?

ANYTUS:

By Heracles, Socrates, forbear! I only hope that no friend or kinsman or acquaintance of mine, whether citizen or stranger, will ever be so mad as to allow himself to be corrupted by them; for they are a manifest pest and corrupting influence to those who have to do with them.

SOCRATES:

What, Anytus? Of all the people who profess that they know how to do men good, do you mean to say that these are the only ones who not only do them no good, but positively corrupt those who are entrusted to them, and in return for this disservice have the face to demand money? Indeed, I cannot believe you; for I know of a single man, Protagoras, who made more out of his craft than the illustrious Pheidias, who created such noble works, or any ten other statuaries. How could that be? A mender of old shoes, or patcher up of clothes, who made the shoes or clothes worse than he received them, could not have remained thirty days undetected, and would very soon have starved; whereas during more than forty years, Protagoras was corrupting all Hellas, and sending his disciples from him worse than he received them, and he was never found out. For, if I am not mistaken, he was about seventy years old at his death, forty of which were spent in the practice of his profession; and during all that time he had a good reputation, which to this day he retains: and not only Protagoras, but many others are well spoken of; some who lived before him, and others who are still living. Now, when you say that they deceived and corrupted the youth, are they to be supposed to have corrupted them consciously or unconsciously? Can those who were deemed by many to be the wisest men of Hellas have been out of their minds?

ANYTUS:

Out of their minds! No, Socrates; the young men who gave their money to them were out of their minds, and their relations and guardians who entrusted their youth to the care of these men were still more out of their minds, and most of all, the cities who allowed them to come in, and did not drive them out, citizen and stranger alike.

SOCRATES:

Has any of the Sophists wronged you, Anytus? What makes you so angry with them?

ANYTUS:

No, indeed, neither I nor any of my belongings has ever had, nor would I suffer them to have, anything to do with them.

SOCRATES:

Then you are entirely unacquainted with them?

ANYTUS:

And I have no wish to be acquainted.

SOCRATES:

Then, my dear friend, how can you know whether a thing is good or bad of which you are wholly ignorant?

ANYTUS:

Quite well; I am sure that I know what manner of men these are, whether I am acquainted with them or not.

SOCRATES:

You must be a diviner, Anytus, for I really cannot make out, judging from your own words, how, if you are not acquainted with them, you know about them. But I am not enquiring of you who are the teachers who will corrupt Meno (let them be, if you please, the Sophists); I only ask you to tell him who there is in this great city who will teach him how to become eminent in the virtues which I was just now describing. He is the friend of your family, and you will oblige him.

ANYTUS:

Why do you not tell him yourself?

SOCRATES:

I have told him whom I supposed to be the teachers of these things; but I learn from you that I am utterly at fault, and I dare say that you are right. And now I wish that you, on your part, would tell me to whom among the Athenians he should go. Whom would you name?

ANYTUS:

Why single out individuals? Any Athenian gentleman, taken at random, if he will mind him, will do far more good to him than the Sophists.

SOCRATES:

And did those gentlemen grow of themselves; and without having been taught by any one, were they nevertheless able to teach others that which they had never learned themselves?

ANYTUS:

I imagine that they learned of the previous generation of gentlemen. Have there not been many good men in this city?

SOCRATES:

Yes, certainly, Anytus; and many good statesmen also there always have been and there are still, in the city of Athens. But the question is whether they were also good teachers of their own virtue;—not whether there are, or have been, good men in this part of the world, but whether virtue can be taught, is the question which we have been discussing. Now, do we mean to say that the good men of our own and of other times knew how to impart to others that virtue which they had themselves; or is virtue a thing incapable of being communicated or imparted by one man to another? That is the question which I and Meno have been arguing. Look at the matter in your own way: Would you not admit that Themistocles was a good man?

ANYTUS:

Certainly; no man better.

SOCRATES:

And must not he then have been a good teacher, if any man ever was a good teacher, of his own virtue?

ANYTUS:

Yes certainly,—if he wanted to be so.

SOCRATES:

But would he not have wanted? He would, at any rate, have desired to make his own son a good man and a gentleman; he could not have been jealous of him, or have intentionally abstained from imparting to him his own virtue. Did you never hear that he made his son Cleophantus a famous horseman; and had him taught to stand upright on horseback and hurl a javelin, and to do many other marvellous things; and in anything which could be learned from a master he was well trained? Have you not heard from our elders of him?

ANYTUS:

I have.

SOCRATES:

Then no one could say that his son showed any want of capacity?

ANYTUS:

Very likely not.

SOCRATES:

But did any one, old or young, ever say in your hearing that Cleophantus, son of Themistocles, was a wise or good man, as his father was?

ANYTUS:

I have certainly never heard any one say so.

SOCRATES:

And if virtue could have been taught, would his father Themistocles have sought to train him in these minor accomplishments, and allowed him who, as you must remember, was his own son, to be no better than his neighbours in those qualities in which he himself excelled?

ANYTUS:

Indeed, indeed, I think not.

SOCRATES:

Here was a teacher of virtue whom you admit to be among the best men of the past. Let us take another,—Aristides, the son of Lysimachus: would you not acknowledge that he was a good man?

ANYTUS:

To be sure I should.

SOCRATES:

And did not he train his son Lysimachus better than any other Athenian in all that could be done for him by the help of masters? But what has been the result? Is he a bit better than any other mortal? He is an acquaintance of yours, and you see what he is like. There is Pericles, again, magnificent in his wisdom; and he, as you are aware, had two sons, Paralus and Xanthippus.

ANYTUS:

I know.

SOCRATES:

And you know, also, that he taught them to be unrivalled horsemen, and had them trained in music and gymnastics and all sorts of arts—in these respects they were on a level with the best—and had he no wish to make good men of them? Nay, he must have wished it. But virtue, as I suspect, could not be taught. And that you may not suppose the incompetent teachers to be only the meaner sort of Athenians and few in number, remember again that Thucydides had two sons, Melesias and Stephanus, whom, besides giving them a good education in other things, he trained in wrestling, and they were the best wrestlers in Athens: one of them he committed to the care of Xanthias, and the other of Eudorus, who had the reputation of being the most celebrated wrestlers of that day. Do you remember them?

ANYTUS:

I have heard of them.

SOCRATES:

Now, can there be a doubt that Thucydides, whose children were taught things for which he had to spend money, would have taught them to be good men, which would have cost him nothing, if virtue could have been taught? Will you reply that he was a mean man, and had not many friends among the Athenians and allies? Nay, but he was of a great family, and a man of influence at Athens and in all Hellas, and, if virtue could have been taught, he would have found out some Athenian or foreigner who would have made good men of his sons, if he could not himself spare the time from cares of state. Once more, I suspect, friend Anytus, that virtue is not a thing which can be taught?

ANYTUS:

Socrates, I think that you are too ready to speak evil of men: and, if you will take my advice, I would recommend you to be careful. Perhaps there is no city in which it is not easier to do men harm than to do them good, and this is certainly the case at Athens, as I believe that you know.

SOCRATES:

O Meno, think that Anytus is in a rage. And he may well be in a rage, for he thinks, in the first place, that I am defaming these gentlemen; and in the second place, he is of opinion that he is one of them himself. But some day he will know what is the meaning of defamation, and if he ever does, he will forgive me. Meanwhile I will return to you, Meno; for I suppose that there are gentlemen in your region too?

MENO:

Certainly there are.

SOCRATES:

And are they willing to teach the young? and do they profess to be teachers? and do they agree that virtue is taught?

MENO:

No indeed, Socrates, they are anything but agreed; you may hear them saying at one time that virtue can be taught, and then again the reverse.

SOCRATES:

Can we call those teachers who do not acknowledge the possibility of their own vocation?

MENO:

I think not, Socrates.

SOCRATES:

And what do you think of these Sophists, who are the only professors? Do they seem to you to be teachers of virtue?

MENO:

I often wonder, Socrates, that Gorgias is never heard promising to teach virtue: and when he hears others promising he only laughs at them; but he thinks that men should be taught to speak.

SOCRATES:

Then do you not think that the Sophists are teachers?

MENO:

I cannot tell you, Socrates; like the rest of the world, I am in doubt, and sometimes I think that they are teachers and sometimes not.

SOCRATES:

And are you aware that not you only and other politicians have doubts whether virtue can be taught or not, but that Theognis the poet says the very same thing?

MENO:

Where does he say so?

SOCRATES:

In these elegiac verses (Theog.):

'Eat and drink and sit with the mighty, and make yourself agreeable to them; for from the good you will learn what is good, but if you mix with the bad you will lose the intelligence which you already have.'

Do you observe that here he seems to imply that virtue can be taught?

MENO:

Clearly.

SOCRATES:

But in some other verses he shifts about and says (Theog.):

'If understanding could be created and put into a man, then they' (who were able to perform this feat) 'would have obtained great rewards.'

And again:—

'Never would a bad son have sprung from a good sire, for he would have heard the voice of instruction; but not by teaching will you ever make a bad man into a good one.'

And this, as you may remark, is a contradiction of the other.

MENO:

Clearly.

SOCRATES:

And is there anything else of which the professors are affirmed not only not to be teachers of others, but to be ignorant themselves, and bad at the knowledge of that which they are professing to teach? or is there anything about which even the acknowledged 'gentlemen' are sometimes saying that 'this thing can be taught,' and sometimes the opposite? Can you say that they are teachers in any true sense whose ideas are in such confusion?

MENO:

I should say, certainly not.

SOCRATES:

But if neither the Sophists nor the gentlemen are teachers, clearly there can be no other teachers?

MENO:

No.

SOCRATES:

And if there are no teachers, neither are there disciples?

MENO:

Agreed.

SOCRATES:

And we have admitted that a thing cannot be taught of which there are neither teachers nor disciples?

MENO:

We have.

SOCRATES:

And there are no teachers of virtue to be found anywhere?

MENO:

There are not.

SOCRATES:

And if there are no teachers, neither are there scholars?

MENO:

That, I think, is true.

SOCRATES:

Then virtue cannot be taught?

MENO:

Not if we are right in our view. But I cannot believe, Socrates, that there are no good men: And if there are, how did they come into existence?

SOCRATES:

I am afraid, Meno, that you and I are not good for much, and that Gorgias has been as poor an educator of you as Prodicus has been of me. Certainly we shall have to look to ourselves, and try to find some one who will help in some way or other to improve us. This I say, because I observe that in the previous discussion none of us remarked that right and good action is possible to man under other guidance than that of knowledge (episteme);—and indeed if this be denied, there is no seeing how there can be any good men at all.

MENO:

How do you mean, Socrates?

SOCRATES:

I mean that good men are necessarily useful or profitable. Were we not right in admitting this? It must be so.

MENO:

Yes.

SOCRATES:

And in supposing that they will be useful only if they are true guides to us of action—there we were also right?

MENO:

Yes.

SOCRATES:

But when we said that a man cannot be a good guide unless he have knowledge (phrhonesis), this we were wrong.

MENO:

What do you mean by the word 'right'?

SOCRATES:

I will explain. If a man knew the way to Larisa, or anywhere else, and went to the place and led others thither, would he not be a right and good guide?

MENO:

Certainly.

SOCRATES:

And a person who had a right opinion about the way, but had never been and did not know, might be a good guide also, might he not?

MENO:

Certainly.

SOCRATES:

And while he has true opinion about that which the other knows, he will be just as good a guide if he thinks the truth, as he who knows the truth?

MENO:

Exactly.

SOCRATES:

Then true opinion is as good a guide to correct action as knowledge; and that was the point which we omitted in our speculation about the nature of virtue, when we said that knowledge only is the guide of right action; whereas there is also right opinion.

MENO:

True.

SOCRATES:

Then right opinion is not less useful than knowledge?

MENO:

The difference, Socrates, is only that he who has knowledge will always be right; but he who has right opinion will sometimes be right, and sometimes not.

SOCRATES:

What do you mean? Can he be wrong who has right opinion, so long as he has right opinion?

MENO:

I admit the cogency of your argument, and therefore, Socrates, I wonder that knowledge should be preferred to right opinion—or why they should ever differ.

SOCRATES:

And shall I explain this wonder to you?

MENO:

Do tell me.

SOCRATES:

You would not wonder if you had ever observed the images of Daedalus (Compare Euthyphro); but perhaps you have not got them in your country?

MENO:

What have they to do with the question?

SOCRATES:

Because they require to be fastened in order to keep them, and if they are not fastened they will play truant and run away.

MENO:

Well, what of that?

SOCRATES:

I mean to say that they are not very valuable possessions if they are at liberty, for they will walk off like runaway slaves; but when fastened, they are of great value, for they are really beautiful works of art. Now this is an illustration of the nature of true opinions: while they abide with us they are beautiful and fruitful, but they run away out of the human soul, and do not remain long, and therefore they are not of much value until they are fastened by the tie of the cause; and this fastening of them, friend Meno, is recollection, as you and I have agreed to call it. But when they are bound, in the first place, they have the nature of knowledge; and, in the second place, they are abiding. And this is why knowledge is more honourable and excellent than true opinion, because fastened by a chain.

MENO:

What you are saying, Socrates, seems to be very like the truth.

SOCRATES:

I too speak rather in ignorance; I only conjecture. And yet that knowledge differs from true opinion is no matter of conjecture with me. There are not many things which I profess to know, but this is most certainly one of them.

MENO:

Yes, Socrates; and you are quite right in saying so.

SOCRATES:

And am I not also right in saying that true opinion leading the way perfects action quite as well as knowledge?

MENO:

There again, Socrates, I think you are right.

SOCRATES:

Then right opinion is not a whit inferior to knowledge, or less useful in action; nor is the man who has right opinion inferior to him who has knowledge?

MENO:

True.

SOCRATES:

And surely the good man has been acknowledged by us to be useful?

MENO:

Yes.

SOCRATES:

Seeing then that men become good and useful to states, not only because they have knowledge, but because they have right opinion, and that neither knowledge nor right opinion is given to man by nature or acquired by him—(do you imagine either of them to be given by nature?

MENO:

Not I.)

SOCRATES:

Then if they are not given by nature, neither are the good by nature good?

MENO:

Certainly not.

SOCRATES:

And nature being excluded, then came the question whether virtue is acquired by teaching?

MENO:

Yes.

SOCRATES:

If virtue was wisdom (or knowledge), then, as we thought, it was taught?

MENO:

Yes.

SOCRATES:

And if it was taught it was wisdom?

MENO:

Certainly.

SOCRATES:

And if there were teachers, it might be taught; and if there were no teachers, not?

MENO:

True.

SOCRATES:

But surely we acknowledged that there were no teachers of virtue?

MENO:

Yes.

SOCRATES:

Then we acknowledged that it was not taught, and was not wisdom?

MENO:

Certainly.

SOCRATES:

And yet we admitted that it was a good?

MENO:

Yes.

SOCRATES:

And the right guide is useful and good?

MENO:

Certainly.

SOCRATES:

And the only right guides are knowledge and true opinion—these are the guides of man; for things which happen by chance are not under the guidance of man: but the guides of man are true opinion and knowledge.

MENO:

I think so too.

SOCRATES:

But if virtue is not taught, neither is virtue knowledge.

MENO:

Clearly not.

SOCRATES:

Then of two good and useful things, one, which is knowledge, has been set aside, and cannot be supposed to be our guide in political life.

MENO:

I think not.

SOCRATES:

And therefore not by any wisdom, and not because they were wise, did Themistocles and those others of whom Anytus spoke govern states. This was the reason why they were unable to make others like themselves—because their virtue was not grounded on knowledge.

MENO:

That is probably true, Socrates.

SOCRATES:

But if not by knowledge, the only alternative which remains is that statesmen must have guided states by right opinion, which is in politics what divination is in religion; for diviners and also prophets say many things truly, but they know not what they say.

MENO:

So I believe.

SOCRATES:

And may we not, Meno, truly call those men 'divine' who, having no understanding, yet succeed in many a grand deed and word?

MENO:

Certainly.

SOCRATES:

Then we shall also be right in calling divine those whom we were just now speaking of as diviners and prophets, including the whole tribe of poets. Yes, and statesmen above all may be said to be divine and illumined, being inspired and possessed of God, in which condition they say many grand things, not knowing what they say.

MENO:

Yes.

SOCRATES:

And the women too, Meno, call good men divine—do they not? and the Spartans, when they praise a good man, say 'that he is a divine man.'

MENO:

And I think, Socrates, that they are right; although very likely our friend Anytus may take offence at the word.

SOCRATES:

I do not care; as for Anytus, there will be another opportunity of talking with him. To sum up our enquiry—the result seems to be, if we are at all right in our view, that virtue is neither natural nor acquired, but an instinct given by God to the virtuous. Nor is the instinct accompanied by reason, unless there may be supposed to be among statesmen some one who is capable of educating statesmen. And if there be such an one, he may be said to be among the living what Homer says that Tiresias was among the dead, 'he alone has understanding; but the rest are flitting shades'; and he and his virtue in like manner will be a reality among shadows.

MENO:

That is excellent, Socrates.

SOCRATES:

Then, Meno, the conclusion is that virtue comes to the virtuous by the gift of God. But we shall never know the certain truth until, before asking how virtue is given, we enquire into the actual nature of virtue. I fear that I must go away, but do you, now that you are persuaded yourself, persuade our friend Anytus. And do not let him be so exasperated; if you can conciliate him, you will have done good service to the Athenian people.